A Braid Society Exhibition

BRAIDS & BEYOND

A BROAD LOOK AT NARROW WARES

Designed and curated by:

Jacqui Carey

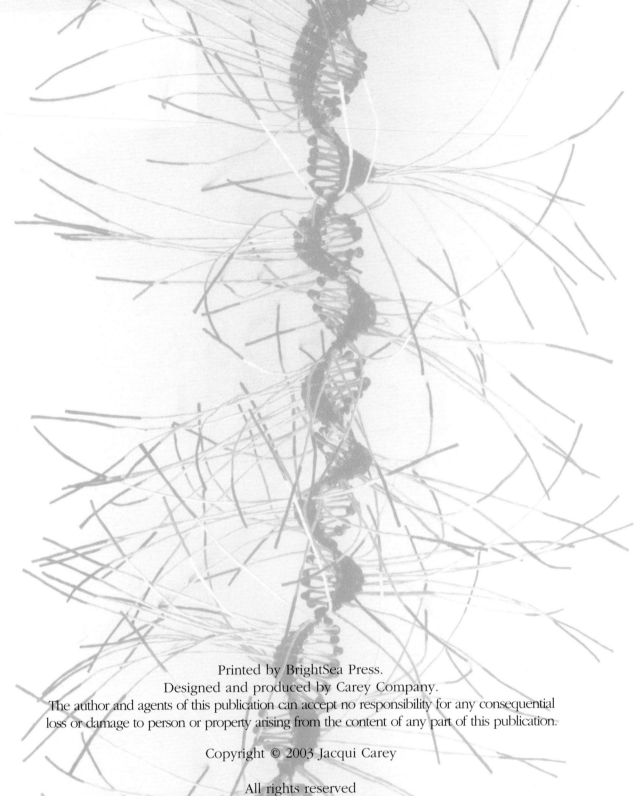

Printed by BrightSea Press.
Designed and produced by Carey Company.
The author and agents of this publication can accept no responsibility for any consequential
loss or damage to person or property arising from the content of any part of this publication.

ISBN 0 9523225 4 4

Acknowledgements

A project like this would not be possible without the generous assistance given by so many people. Our thanks goes to all of those who kindly lent objects for the duration of the exhibition, also to those who have allowed us to use the images that have added an extra dimension. Particular thanks goes to the curators and staff of the following museums and collections: Bowes Museum; Carrow House, Costume and Textile Study Centre; Newarke Houses Museum; Royal Albert Memorial Museum; Royal College of Obstetricians and Gynaecologists; Saffron Walden Museum; the Wade Costume Collection, Snowshill Manor (the National Trust); and Wigan Archives.

Support has also been provided by the following: Heritage Lottery Fund; Joan Howes Trust; Creative Exhibitions; Handweavers Studio; Association of Guilds; Silken Strands; Toye, Kenning & Spencer Ltd; Eaton Ltd; Parker Hannifin plc; and Pearsalls Ltd.

The body of information that has accumulated over the centuries has been made possible by the dedicated study of many people. Various contributors have helped with this aspect of the exhibition, and specific mention should go to the following: Jenny Balfour-Paul, Europa Chang, Peter Collingwood, Gina Corrigan, Anna Crutchley, Claude Delmas, Eiluned Edwards, Ruth Gilbert, Masako Kinoshita, Althea MacKenzie, Linda Mowat, Ray Napier, Ann Norman, Des Pawson, Errol Pires, Len Pole, Lise Raeder Knudsen, Nina Sparr, Noemi Speiser.

Thanks should also go to members of the Braid Society for their support, and to Carey Company for production work and Geoff Hudson for the poster design.

Jan Rawdon Smith (Chair) and the team:
Jacqui Carey (Curator), Anne Dyer, Edna Gibson and Veronica Johnston.

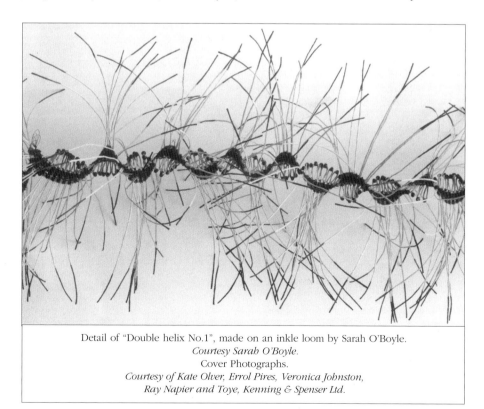

Detail of "Double helix No.1", made on an inkle loom by Sarah O'Boyle.
Courtesy Sarah O'Boyle.
Cover Photographs.
Courtesy of Kate Olver, Errol Pires, Veronica Johnston,
Ray Napier and Toye, Kenning & Spenser Ltd.

Detail of braids and cords forming the structure of a raincloak from Burma.
Courtesy of Royal Albert Memorial Museum.

Introduction

In 1993, the Braid Society held its inaugural meeting in London, bringing together people interested in the world of braids and narrow wares. Since then the Society has been a focal point for the exchange of information. Workshops, study days, exhibitions, newsletters and a yearly journal have helped to fulfil part of its aim, to promote the understanding and practice of this area of textiles. This exhibition, celebrating our 10th birthday, aims to continue this work by highlighting some of the ways of making and using narrow wares, with the intention of showing that the term covers a broad range of interesting textiles.

What is a braid ?

We often use the word *braid* informally, to describe a textile that is narrow in proportion to its length, irrespective of its method of construction. However, when the term is used in a more specialised context, it takes on new meaning.

Terminology is a debatable issue in all fields of study, and textiles are no exception. With the increase in global communication, it would seem sensible for definitions to be consistent, and attempts have been made to create definitive terminologies. But the richness of our language offers us a complex choice of words, stemming from a multitude of roots.

Under normal circumstances the understanding of a term is absorbed from the everyday familiarity of one's environment and in general consensus with the people in it. But language is dynamic, and the meaning of words changes through time, over distance and between social groups. For example, in the past, a *braided* textile was one that had faded in colour, an interpretation that is obsolete today. People from different parts of the world use terms in different ways. For example, in India, the western term of *ply split braiding* has no direct translation. The makers of this traditional technique make no distinction between their braiding and weaving, calling both techniques *gunthana*. There are occupational differences too. In many UK fishing communities *braiding* is understood as the technique used to make new knotted nets; whilst neighbouring hairdressers would interpret the word as a way of creating a particular hairstyle.

The problem is not just in understanding the meaning of a term but also in deciding where the boundaries lie, for example, how wide is narrow ?

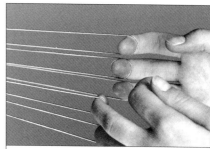

Terminology varies over time. In the 17th Century these would be referred to as *boes*, whilst today they are called *loops*.

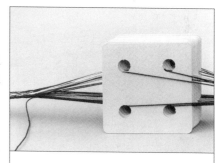

Terminology varies over distance. In Britain this is called *tabletweaving*, but in America it is known as *cardweaving*.

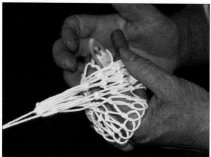

Terminology varies between social groups. The craftspeople who hand-make billiard pockets refer to their work as *braiding*, whilst others call it *knotting*.
Courtesy of Elizabeth Wright and Redport Net Limited.

Definitions can be used to avoid problems in communication. But even when precise definitions are stated, there may still be differences of opinion and interpretation. For example, Irene Emery and Noémi Speiser, both regarded as authorities on terminology, define braiding in the following manner: Speiser defines braiding as "interworking a set of elements* by crossing, interlacing, interlinking, twining, intertwining..." (*The Manual of Braiding*), whilst Emery separates the interworking of a set of elements into interlinking, oblique interlacing, oblique twining and interknotting, placing *braiding* as synonymous only with oblique interlacing (*The Primary Structures of Fabric*).

There are many more, equally valid definitions. So, although we may recognise the similarities and differences between things, how we choose to group and label them will always be subjective.

(*Note: *element* refers to a working unit, eg thread, yarn, strip, strand etc)

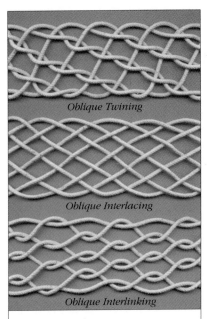

Oblique Twining

Oblique Interlacing

Oblique Interlinking

Using Noémi Speiser's definition, all of these are examples made using the technique of *braiding*, whilst Irene Emery defines just the oblique interlacing as an example of *braiding*.

This *warp-twining* structure can be produced using different techniques.

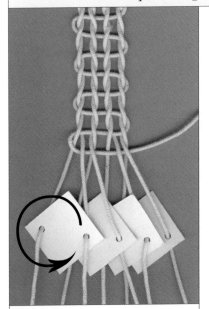

Tablet weaving.
The tablets are turned as a pack to create a *shed*, through which the weft can pass.

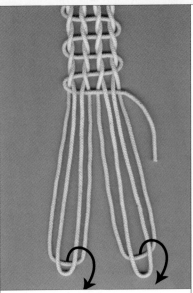

Loop-manipulating.
Pairs of loops are worked together so that one loop is taken through its partner. This creates a shed through which the weft can pass.

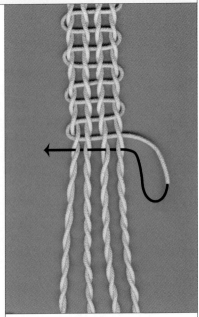

Ply-splitting.
A weft thread is taken between the plies of twisted cords.

Identification

There are many different types of narrow wares, which can be grouped in a variety of ways. For example they can be divided according to: the technique used to create them (e.g. weaving, knitting,); the structure (e.g. interlaced, interlinked); their country of origin (e.g. Japan, Peru,); their purpose or function (e.g. slings, purse strings); even by the materials used to produce them (e.g. silk, straw).

Classification by technique focuses on the activity (the method of production), rather than the result (the final structure). This is a popular way of categorising narrow wares, and it is the most relevant to practising craftspeople. However, when looking at a finished product, it can be difficult to identify the technique with any certainty. This is because there are different ways of achieving the same result (see images on opposite page). Therefore, identification by technique has to be backed up by other evidence. The idiosyncrasies of each method can offer clues, as can ethnographic research. Surprisingly, some of the best evidence comes from mistakes made during production.

When studying a finished product, it seems more obvious to classify by structure because the focus is on the actual properties of the piece. However, problems can still arise if evidence is missing. Unfortunately, textiles do not always survive intact, and fragments can be misleading (see images below)

So, for all forms of identification, it is important to keep in mind what is actually known and what is assumed, and to remember that;

One technique can produce different structures and a single structure can be produced using different techniques.

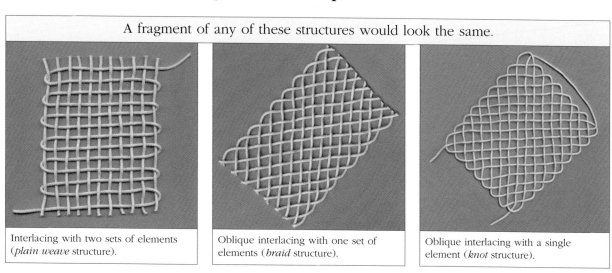

A fragment of any of these structures would look the same.

Interlacing with two sets of elements (*plain weave* structure).	Oblique interlacing with one set of elements (*braid* structure).	Oblique interlacing with a single element (*knot* structure).

Twisting

Twisting elements* together to produce a cord is usually done in two stages. The first stage is to individually twist two or more elements in the same direction. These elements are then twisted together in the opposite direction. The twists create opposing forces that hold the structure together.

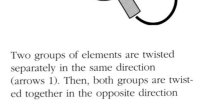

Here, the word twisting is used to describe an action, but it can also be used specifically when the process is applied to un-spun elements. Plying is then used to describe the process done with elements made from spun yarn.

The twisting process can be applied many times to add strength and thickness to the finished product. The technique has been applied to all kinds of materials and the underlying principle is same, at any scale, from the making of fine sewing threads to huge cables for ships. It is distinctly different from *spinning*, a method that twists together short fibres to form a single continuous length. However, confusion can arise between the two techniques as the word *spinning* is used by the passementerie industry to describe their cordmaking.

Evidence of an S-twist, cord has been discovered in France, in the Lascaux caves, dating from 15,000BC. This illustrates that twisting is one of the earliest of textile techniques. It is also a widespread one, and many different methods of production have evolved throughout the world. It is not necessary to use equipment to make a cord; rolling threads between two palms, or between a palm and thigh, is sufficient

Two groups of elements are twisted separately in the same direction (arrows 1). Then, both groups are twisted together in the opposite direction (arrow 2).

From top to bottom: a *2-ply, 3-ply* and *4-ply* cord. The numbers indicate how many elements were used to create each cord.

to produce a twisting action. However, various tools have been developed to help speed up the process. Any device that is used for spinning, such as a spindle or spinning wheel, can be used to twist or ply threads together.

*In this context, *element* refers to a working unit that can consist of one or more *threads* (where *thread* represents any yarn, strand, filament etc of any pliable material, type or scale).

Left: if the final twist is in a clockwise direction, the cord is known as *S-twist* (because the diagonal slant follows the central slant of the letter S).
Right: if the final twist is in an anti-clockwise direction, the cord is known as *Z-twist* (because the diagonal slant follows the central slant of the letter Z).

Suspension cord.
Courtesy of Anna Crutchley.

A Tibetan nomad in China using a devise for twisting
Photograph by Nick Hodgson.
Courtesy of Susi Dunsmore.

The principle can be applied at any scale, from the making of fine sewing threads to large ropes.
Courtesy of Des Pawson.

Ahmoud, a Tuareg guide, making a camel hobble in the Sahara. He is twisting the date-palm fibre between his hands.
Courtesy of Veronica Johnston.

Other tools have been specifically designed for plying, such as the *jack*. This device consists of a rack of hooks connected to a handle. Each hook holds the end of one element while the other ends are brought together and attached to a swivel on another post. The handle simultaneously turns each hook on its own axis, thus twisting the elements. When sufficient twist has been transferred to the individual elements, they can all be twisted together. This type of equipment is used in both the ropemaking and passementerie industry.

Front and side view of an 18th Century *jack*. It is still used occasionally in the passementerie industry.
Courtesy of Leicester City Museum Services.

Replica tassel made for Polesden Lacey, Dorking, Surrey, by Anna Crutchley. A variety of passementerie *cordspinning* techniques have been used in the suspension cord, tassel mould coverings, and overskirt.
Courtesy of Anna Crutchley.

How to make a 2-ply, Z-twist cord.

Step 1.
Knot together two bundles of thread, in this case, one group of blue threads and another group of navy (each containing six strands of cotton perle).

Step 2.
Secure these threads to a post and start twisting one bundle of threads in a clockwise direction. Keep twisting until the threads start to pucker (the more twist you put in the threads, the tighter the final result will be).

Step 3.
Secure these twisted threads so that they do not unravel. Here, they have been sticky taped to the table. Note that they are shorter in length than the untwisted threads.
Now, twist the other group of threads in a clockwise direction.

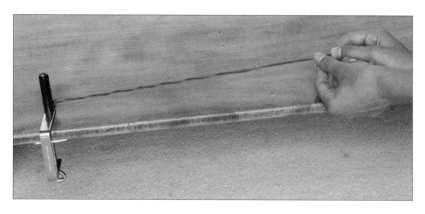

Step 4.
Take both groups of threads and twist them together in an anti-clockwise direction.
Secure the end to finish.

Knotting

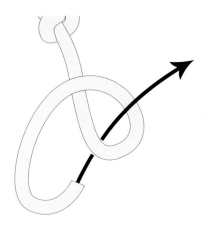

Broadly speaking, knotting is a technique that tightens elements that have been taken through loops, formed by themselves or other elements. However, specialists differentiate between a *knot* as being worked with just one element, whilst a *bend* is worked with two elements, and a *hitch* is formed by one element over another inert element.

The primary function of a knot is utilitarian, but knotting has also been developed for more aesthetic purposes, including the making of narrow wares. One particular method consists of a series of overhand knots tied in a length of thread with the aid of a shuttle. These fine knotted cords were then couched down to form decorative patterns on clothing or furnishings, or gathered into loops for fringing. This style of work was popular in the 17th Century but it eventually evolved into the more intricate technique of tatting.

Balls of knotting (right) made with shuttles (above). This type of knotting was a popular and genteel pastime in the 17th Century.
Courtesy of Carrow House (Norfolk Museums and Archaeology Service).

A more enduring knotting technique is *macramé*. The name and technique is said to derive from the Arabic *mucharram*. Macramé, also known as *square knotting*, is made from a series of hitches worked over passive threads. It is generally associated with wide fabric, specifically fringes, although it is also used to describe long, narrow sections. It was a popular pastime in the navy during the 19th Century along with other forms of fancy knotwork.

Another form of narrow knotting popular with sailors was *crown sinnet* making. The word *sinnet* is often used to describe narrow wares made using a variety of techniques (interlooping, interlacing etc) but a *crown sinnet* is a specific structure made from a series of knots known as *crowns*. In the second half of the 20th Century, it was made fashionable by working it in plastic tubing and calling it *scoobee doo*.

Knotting is not just favoured for its decorative qualities but also for its ability to hold significant meaning. There are widespread examples of knotting being associated with magical spells, protective talismans and lucky charms. Knotted narrow wares have also been used as a way of communicating or storing information, for example, the knotted cords known as *Quipu* were used by the Incas to keep trading records and accounts.

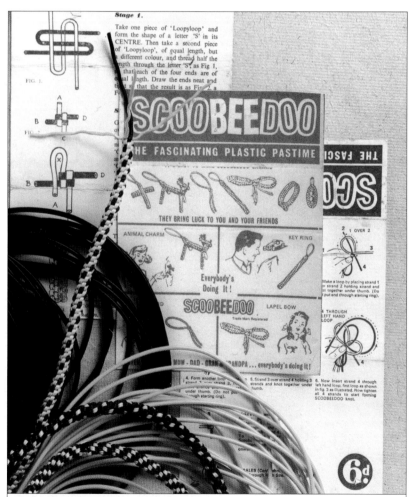

Instruction sheets for *Scoobee doo*, dating from the 1960's and 70's, showing how to make cr*own sinnets* with plastic tubing.
Courtesy of Des Pawson.

Chinese knotting is imbued with meaning. This example expressed good wishes for a farmer's harvest.
Courtesy of Europa Chang.

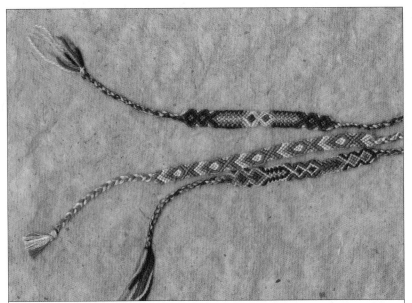

These *friendship* bracelets are made using knotting techniques.
Courtesy of Edna Gibson.

Sailors have long been associated with the technique of knotting, in both its functional and decorative form. Not only was it a necessary skill required for their trade but it also played an important part in their recreation.
Courtesy of Denis Murphy.

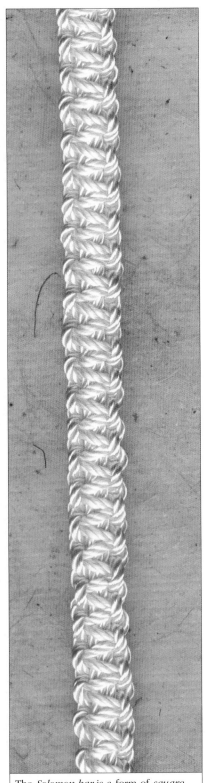

The *Solomon bar* is a form of *square knotting*.

How to make a *Bannister bar*.

Step 1.
Join together four threads (make two of them three times as long as the other two).
Arrange the threads so that the two long ones, known as *workers,* are on the outside and the two short ones, known as *passives,* are on the inside. It may help to wrap the workers into little *butterfly* balls so that they do not tangle.
It is easier to work if the passives threads are held under tension. Here, all of the threads are attached to a post, whilst the ends of the passives are pinned to the worker's trousers.

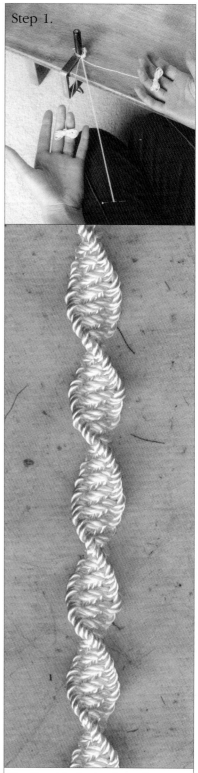

Step 2.
To make a *macramé,* or *half knot,* form a loop with the left-hand worker and take it over the two passives and under the right-hand worker.

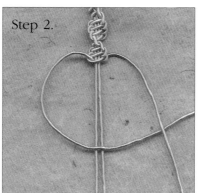

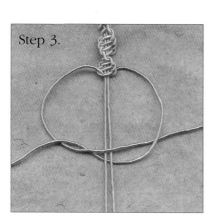

Step 3.
Take the right-hand worker behind the two passives and up through the loop made by the left-hand worker.

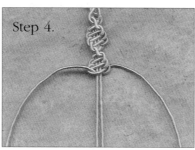

Step 4.
Tighten the knot and repeat the process. Always start on the left-hand side so that the knots gradually twist around the passives.

The *Solomon bar* is made in the same way except that the half-knot is made alternately from the left and right.

The *Bannister bar* is a form of *square knotting.*

Knitting

Knitting is a form of interlooping. It is built up in rows, usually from a single working element. Each row consists of loops, normally held on needles, with subsequent rows being worked by pulling a loop of the working element through a loop from the previous row.

The technique is usually associated with large-scale fabric production. However, it can be used to produce narrow wares. A two-loop form of knitting can easily be made over two fingers, or on a two-pronged tool known as a *lucet, lyre* or *chain fork*. This type of work was once very common and it has been said that, at the end of the 18th Century, most homes contained a lucet. Although many tools have survived, not much remains of the work produced on them. One reason could be that the mundane nature of the products meant that little care was taken to preserve them. Also, if knitting is exposed to abrasive wear, one break in the thread can result in the whole structure unravelling.

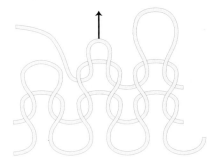

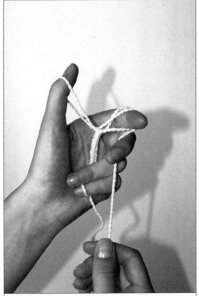

Photograph showing two-looped *cording*, made using instructions from Walter Edmund Roth's written study on the arts and crafts of the Guiana Indians from South America, which was written in the early 1900's

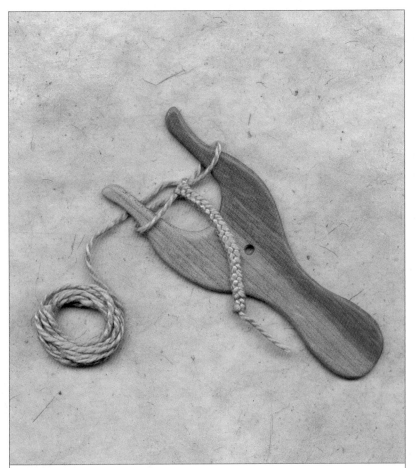

A *lucet* (also known as a *lyre* or *chain fork*) was often used for making everyday functional ties.

A well known example is made on an old cotton reel with nails in the top. It is known by many different names such as *French knitting, corking, knitting Nancy, ratties tails, peg knitting* and *ring knitting*. It usually takes the form of a single thread worked over four pegs, with one loop on each peg. It is often thought of as a child's toy, but it has been used to produce ties, trims and household goods such as coasters. Larger versions, such as the *Moule Turc*, with many pegs around the circumference were used to make fine, tubular knitted bags and purses.

This type of work is known by many names including *French knitting, corking* and *knitting Nancy.*

In the same way that large scale knitting can be worked with several different colours, so too can the narrow versions, with extra twists and turns interworking and exchanging the coloured elements.

This tool, known as a *Moule Turc*, works on the same principle as French knitting but has many more nails.
Courtesy of Carrow House (Norfolk Museums and Archaeology Service).

Belts made from tubular knitting interlaced through a flat laddered section.
Courtesy of Melissa Warren.

A knitted bag with a knitted handle, circa 1870.
Courtesy of Leicester City Museum Services.

How to use a lucet.

Step 1.

With your left hand, hold the start of the thread against the back of the lucet and wrap the thread in a figure of eight around the prongs (you will need to hold the start of the thread for several repeats before it is stable).

Step 1.

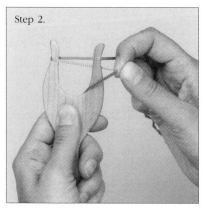

Step 2.

Step 2.

Hold the working end of the thread with your middle to little fingers behind the right-hand prong. With your thumb and index finger pick up the lower loop of thread.

Step 3.

Lift the lower loop over the working end and off the prong, so that the working end forms a new loop.

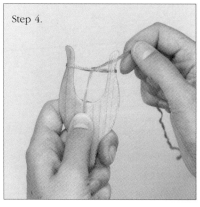

Step 4.

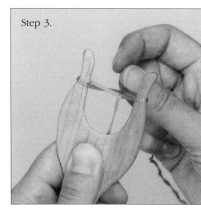

Step 3.

Step 4.

Turn the lucet over in the palm of your left hand, so that the right-hand prong goes over the left-hand one. Pull the working end towards the right, tightening the stitch and making sure that it is central. Take the working end over the end of the right-hand prong ready to start again.

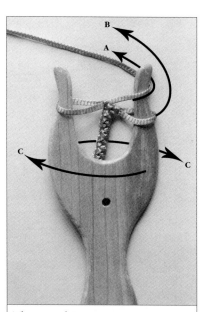

The working sequence can be summarised as:
A. Take the working end around the top of the right-hand prong.
B. Lift the lower loop over the working end and off the prong.
C. Turn the lucet and start again.

To finish, secure by taking the end of the thread through the loops on each prong.

Weaving

Weaving is characterised by two sets of elements known as the *warp* and *weft*. The warp threads are usually held under tension and lie parallel to each other; the weft is then interlaced with them, usually at right angles. The technique has a substantial history that probably dates back to well before 6000 BC. Weaving is usually used to produce wide fabric, and it is a debatable matter as to when a piece of weaving qualifies as a narrow ware. Today, industry specifies that the widest *narrow band* is 216mm (8½ inches) in width and that anything above this measurement is done on a *broad loom*.

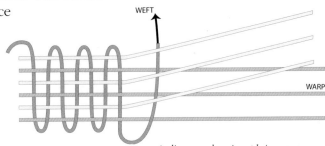

A diagram showing *plain weave*, where the warp and weft interlace *under one, over one*.

Weaving is one of the most frequently used methods of producing narrow wares. It is extremely varied, in both the equipment used to produce it and in the resulting structures. It is possible to weave elements together without any form of support, but this is usually confined to stiff fibres such as those used in mat making and basketry. Softer, more flexible threads benefit from some sort of equipment, usually in the form of a frame for the warp threads. This can be as simple as two sticks placed in the ground or as specialised as a computerised loom.

A strip of *kente* cloth from Ghana, Africa. The *plain weave* structure is distorted to produce alternate *warp-faced* then *weft-faced* fabric. At the top, the green warp threads cover the weft, then the weft of coloured stripes covers the green warp threads.
The yellow squares are created from a *discontinuous supplementary* weft.
Courtesy of Len Pole.

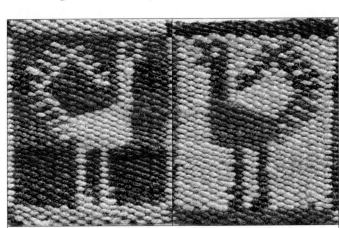

Detail showing the front and back of a belt from Peru. This is an example of *double-cloth*, where two layers of warp threads are worked simultaneously. In this instance, a white layer and a striped coloured layer are interworked to create animal motifs, with the reverse image appearing on the opposite side.
Courtesy of Eiluned Edwards.

Weaving the weft between the warp threads can be achieved simply by pushing down or lifting up individual warp threads as the weft passes through. But a more efficient method is to use *shed sticks, leashes* or *heddles*. These are used to raise or lower a selection of warp threads in unison so that the weft can easily pass through the space created, known as the *shed*.

Narrow bands, made from gold threads, are used to indicate rank on this military shoulder strap.
Courtesy of Toye, Kenning & Spencer Ltd.

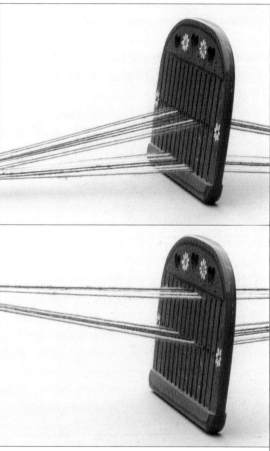

A Swedish rigid heddle used in the production of narrow bands. When the heddle is lifted, some warp threads are raised to create a *shed*. When the heddle is lowered, a new shed is formed for the weft to pass through.
Courtesy of Shirley Berlin.

Backstrap weaving is a method often associated with the production of narrow woven textiles. It is a low-tech way of working and has developed in various forms throughout the world. One end of the warp is secured to a fixed point, such as a post, tree or the feet of the weaver. The other end is attached to a belt around the weaver's waist. Despite the simple nature of the equipment, the results can be remarkably complex, as can be seen in the woven bands from South America.

Some equipment has been developed specifically for making narrow woven fabric. An example of this is the inkle loom. This is a small and portable piece of wooden apparatus that holds a circular warp. It was developed for the manufacture of *inkles*. These were used as garment ties such as garters and stays, as well as for decorative trims on clothes and furnishings.

Opposite: A Peruvian lady backstrap weaving. The warp threads are tensioned between a post in the ground and the belt around her waist. Above: The detail shows the smooth stick holding open the shed through which the weft has passed. *Courtesy of Margaret Potts.*

An inkle loom was developed especially for making narrow woven bands known as *inkles*. *Courtesy of Edna Gibson.*

The headdress on the right belongs to a young, unmarried Ulo Akha woman from Thailand. It is decorated with coins, beads, pom-poms and feather tassels. There are also woven decorations attached at the back (detail shown below).

The woman (above) is making a feather tassel on a bow-loom. She is wearing a more elaborate headdress that signifies her mature status.

Courtesy of Ray Napier.

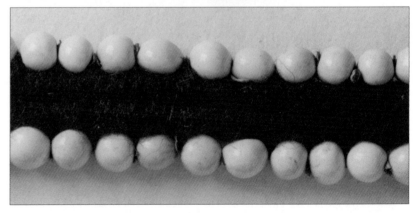

How to make an Akha hat decoration.

Step 1.
Tension and secure four warps, two of which have beads threaded onto them.
The Akha use warp threads of hand-spun cotton threaded with Job's tears and secured on a bamboo bow loom. If you wish, you can use other threads and beads, attaching them between two posts.

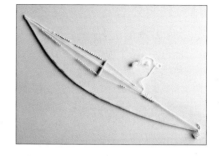

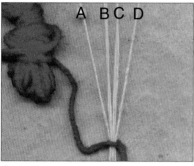

Step 2.
Tie a woollen weft thread onto the warps and start with it on the left. Arrange the warps so that the beads are on the outside ones and mentally label the warps A,B,C and D.

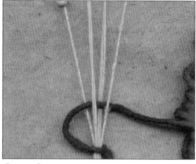

Step 3.
Weave the weft through the warps, going over A, under B, over C and under D.

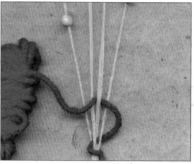

Step 4.
Weave back through three warps, going over D, under C and over B

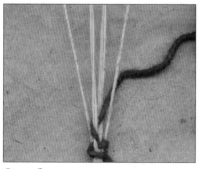

Step 5.
Taking the weft between A and B, weave through two warps, going under B and over C.

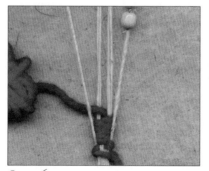

Step 6.
Weave back and forth through two warps (B and C) until the weaving is the height of two beads. As this is a *weft-faced plain weave*, pack the weft down so that it covers the warp threads.

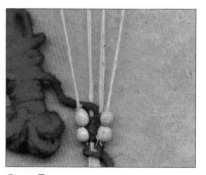

Step 7.
Push down two beads from warp A and D so that they sit alongside the weaving on B and C.
Now you can repeat the sequence from step 3.

Tablet weaving

Tablet weaving (or cardweaving) is a very specific method of working. It is similar to weaving in that warp threads are set up under tension and a shed is opened, enabling the weft to be inserted between the warp threads. The main difference is that flat *tablets* are used to create the shed. These are usually square with a hole in each corner, although 3-holed triangular, 6-holed hexagonal and other shapes are also used. Examples of old tablets have been found made from wood, bone and leather, whilst more modern versions include playing cards and plastic. A warp thread is inserted through each hole so that, when the tablets are held vertically, the warp threads are at different heights, thus creating a shed. When the tablets are turned, different threads are lifted.

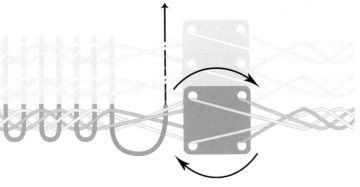

A stylised view of tablet weaving showing how the tablets are used to create a shed. A new shed is formed when the tablets are turned, an action that also twines the warp threads so that they no longer remain parallel to one another.

Tablet weaving in Bhutan. A loom supports the warp threads that are threaded through tablets made from old X-ray plates (see detail above). The worker is holding a smooth wooden stick that is used for beating down the weft.
Courtesy of Veronica Johnston.

Detail showing the distinctive line, and change in the angle of the twine, caused when the tablets are turned in the opposite direction.
Courtesy of Carrow House (Norfolk Museum and Archaeology Services).

This turning puts a twist in the threads so that most of the resulting structures are *warp-twined*, although it is possible to create *plain weave* structures by turning the tablets alternately forwards and backwards. An opposite twist also builds up in the unwoven end of the warp. This can be eliminated by changing the direction of the turn. It makes a distinctive line in the fabric where the warp threads start to twist in the opposite direction.

The tablets are normally turned together as a pack, either in a clockwise or anti-clockwise direction. They can also be turned individually in different combinations. Tablets are usually rotated about their central point, but they can be turned sideways along their horizontal axis. Add to this different ways of threading the tablets, and the use of specialised weaving techniques such as introducing a supplementary weft, and one can see the immense potential of this technique.

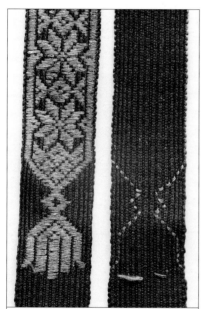

Front and back detail of a *Jerusalem* garter, showing tablet weaving with a *discontinuous supplementary weft*.
A burgundy weft works the main body of the tablet weaving and continues to do so as an additional gold thread is introduced. This gold weft is worked alternately with the burgundy weft to produce the design.
Courtesy of Carrow House (Norfolk Museum and Archaeology Services).

Detail of lettering on a 17th Century garter. Each tablet, threaded with different coloured warps, has been individually turned, either forwards or backwards, to lift the required colour to the surface of the structure.
Courtesy of Carrow House (Norfolk Museum and Archaeology Services).

Tablet weaving has been found in many parts of the world, with different regions developing their own style and patterns, such as the Icelandic *missing hole* work, and the Buddhist symbols found on Tibetan bands.

It is difficult to be certain of the exact development of tablet weaving, but archaeological excavations have unearthed tablets and tablet woven bands from many different areas in Europe. One of the oldest surviving comes from a burial site at Verucchio in Italy and dates from 750BC. Although many early examples were used as the starting border of cloaks made on a vertical loom, the examples from Verucchio appear to have been added to the edge afterwards. They are not stitched down but incorporate the ends of the woven fabric in such a way that the tablet weaving is an integral part of the cloak.

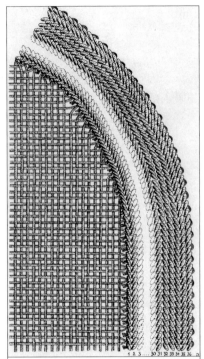

Diagram from the book *"Guerriero E Sacerodote"* showing the band on the cloak from Verucchio.
Courtesy of Lise Raeder Knudsen.

A bracelet made by Lise Raeder Knudsen, from silver and copper tabletweaving.
Courtesy of Lise Raeder Knudsen.

A selection of tablets.
Courtesy of Shirley Berlin.

An 'in-action' view of tablet weaving.

A warp has been prepared so that each thread passes through a 4-holed tablet. Four adjacent threads pass through one tablet, from the same side to the other. The first tablet (fig.1) is *S-threaded* (so that, as you look down on it, the threads slant S-twist). Subsequent tablets alternate Z and S. The warp is tensioned at both ends and a weft is added (fig. 2).

The weft is taken through the first shed and the tablets are rotated a quarter turn forwards, away from the worker (fig. 3). The shed is opened (fig. 4) so that the weft can pass through (fig. 5).

The pack can then be rotated another quarter turn forwards and the process repeated.

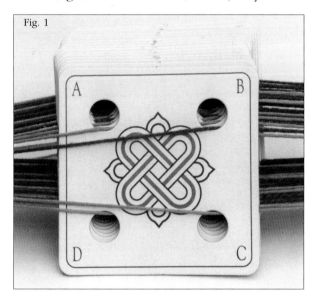

Fig. 1

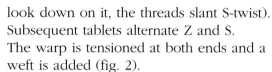

Fig. 2

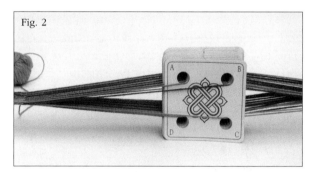

Fig. 3

Fig. 4

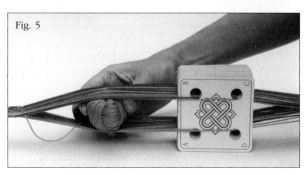

Fig. 5

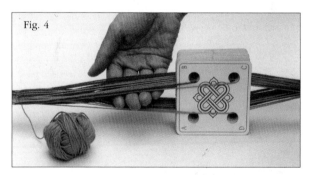

Fig. 6

Courtesy of Edna Gibson.

Free end braiding

Braiding uses a single set of elements worked together at an oblique angle. Free end braiding is a form that requires no equipment. When working, it is easier to have the starting point of the braid secured in some manner. It can simply be held in the hands or between the toes, or it can be tied to a static object such as a tree or post. The braid is built up by manipulating the elements under or over each other so that the work gradually grows away from the fixed end.

Free end braiding is related to mat-making and basketry techniques, and is said to pre-date weaving. The simplest, most fundamental braid is a 3-element one, commonly known as the *pig-tail* braid or plait. It is the most widespread and frequently used braid structure. In general, braid structures create strong products as they bring together several elements in a neat and flexible form.

The absence of equipment makes it a very low-tech and portable method of working, although the practicality of handling many loose threads means that this technique can require considerable dexterity. This is beautifully illustrated in the work by the Dida tribe from Ivory Coast, Africa. Other examples can be found with the *ceinture fléchée* work from Canada and the related braiding from North America.

The 3-element *pig-tail* braid.

Hannah and Bethany having their hair braided by their mother.
Courtesy of the Upchurch family.

Palm-leaf being braided into strips which will be stitched together to form *simah*. These are used to form part of the walls or roof of houses in Oman.
Courtesy of Gigi Crocker Jones.

Detail of a Peruvian sling.
Courtesy of Peter Collingwood.

The Peruvians also have a reputation for dextrous work and they have created a great number of complex braids. Many of these braids are used as slings, traditionally made from alpaca or llama wool. These have also developed into more ceremonial slings that are used as head decorations, belts and accessories for dancing.

Right: A Tibetan nomad making a sling. He holds the growing braid in his left hand whilst his right hand manipulates the free ends. This way of working is also used by the Peruvians.
Above: Finished sling.
Courtesy of Gina Corrigan.

A tie-dyed *skirt* made by the Dida people. Hundreds of fine raffia threads are braided together to form the *tubular, oblique interlaced* structure. Little leashes are used to help create a shed, but all of the manipulation is done by hand.

How to make a 5-element Braid.

This braid is a 5-element version of the *pigtail* braid, worked in three colours. Different patterns can be made by using other combinations and starting positions of colours.

Step 1.
Join together five threads of different colours. Here, the colours are arranged in the following order: yellow, white and yellow held in the left hand; and two blacks held in the right hand.

Step 2.
Take the left most thread in the left hand, to the left most in the right hand (or *outside left to inside right*).

Step 3.
Take the right most thread in the right hand to the right most in the left hand (or *outside right to inside left*).

Continue repeating steps 2 and 3.
The moves can be worked with any odd number of elements. The example below is a 7-element version. A extra element has been added to each group. The moves remain the same - taking the outside to the inside of the opposite group.

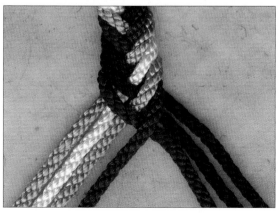

—Stand and bobbin braiding—

The process of stand and bobbin braiding is basically the same as free end braiding, with a single set of elements being interworked, the difference being that equipment is used to support the work.

There are many advantages to using equipment. Bobbins can store large amounts of thread that would inevitably tangle if allowed to hang free. They also support and tension the threads, making it easier to produce more uniform braids than with the free end technique. Using a stand can also help in maintaining the order and position of threads when they are not working. This is particularly useful for complex work when large numbers of elements are involved. The technique involves lifting the bobbins and moving them to a new position in repeatable sequences. Each of these sequences can produce a different structured braid ranging from the basic *pigtail* braid to complex, multi-layered versions.

It is hard to establish the exact origins of stand and bobbin braiding. It has been suggested that braiding with bobbins may date back to prehistoric times but, although weights and bobbin-like objects have been found in excavation, there is no evidence that they were used for braiding. The use of bobbins in lacemaking developed in Europe during the 15th Century, and there are connections between the two techniques. Diderot's encyclopaedia of trades and industry, first written in 1751, illustrates braiding

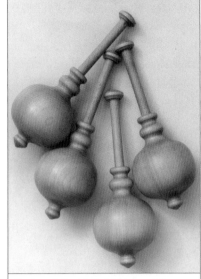

Copies of Danish bobbins used for braidmaking, made by Derrick Earnshaw. They are not used with a stand but are wound with thread and hung from a fixed point so that the bobbins can swing freely.
Courtesy of Gil Dye.

Nina Sparr, from Sweden, is the fifth generation of her family to make hair braids. She is working with human hair wound onto weighted bobbins that rest over a wooden stool known as a *kedjeställning* (chain stand).
Courtesy of Nina Sparr.

Sentimental jewellery made from hair, such as this bracelet, was fashionable during the early Victorian period.
Courtesy of Carrow House (Norfolk Museums and Archaeology Service).

equipment used in the button making trade, and writes about the similarities and differences between these and those used for lacemaking. Equipment was also developed for the making of hair braids, that were used to make fashionable jewellery.

Sample from a 17th Century instruction book showing a braid made using 40 bobbins of the type used for *bone lase* (bone, or bobbin lace). *Courtesy of Wigan Archives Service.*

An illustration from Diderot's encyclopaedia showing two forms of stand and bobbin braiding. The lady on the left is working on a b*oisseau* whilst the man on the right is using a *jatte*. *Courtesy of Leicester City Museum Services.*

Detail of the base of a trouser leg, from Dubai in United Arab Emirates. It is decorated with braids that have been made on a *khajuja*. *Courtesy of Jennifer Aisbitt.*

Equipment developed by Ernie Henshall, from the UK. Bobbins, weighted with washers, are wound with thread and supported over a slotted board on a simple stand. *Courtesy of Jennie Parry.*

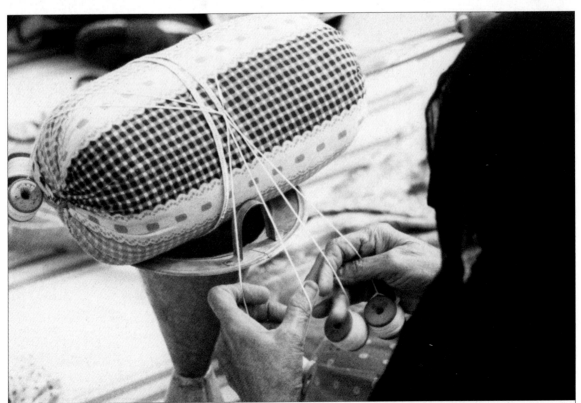

A lady from Oman working on a *khajuja*. She is making a braid with cotton and flat metallic thread that will be used to decorate costume.
Courtesy of Gigi Crocker Jones.

A Miao lady from China working on a wooden stool with bamboo bobbins weighted with coins. She is making a fine silk braid that will be used with embroidery to decorate jackets like the one she is wearing.
Courtesy of Gina Corrigan.

Makiko Tada, from Japan, working on a *takadai* with 288 bobbins. *Courtesy of Makiko Tada.*

Although little remains of the European industry, the technique has had a more resilient tradition in Japan. Here, braiding known as *kumihimo* is made using many different types of equipment, such as the *marudai* and *takadai*. The wearing of *obijime* (the braid worn around kimono) became fashionable in the late 19th Century and this stimulated a prolific trade for handmade silk braids. The trade still continues although it is in decline, as kimonos are no longer considered everyday wear.

Stand and bobbin braiding can also be found elsewhere in the world, but it is not as prevalent as other techniques used for making narrow wares.

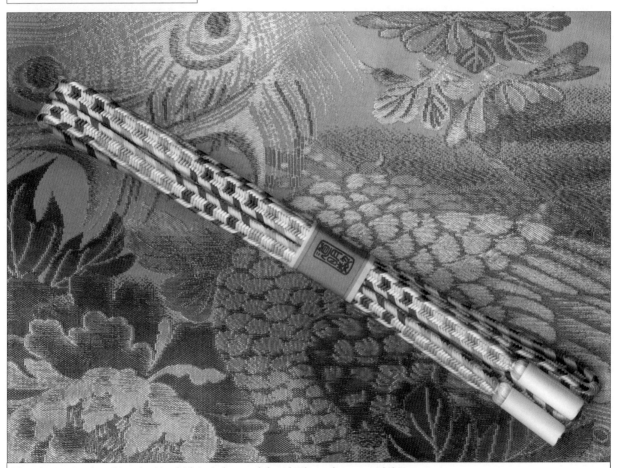

The *obi-jime* is a kumihimo braid, which is tied around the *obi*, the sash worn with kimono.

An 'in-action' view of *kumihimo* worked on a *marudai*.

A marudai is prepared with bundles of fine silk thread (fig.1). The threads have been tied together and attached to the black bag containing counterbalance weights, which hangs below the central hole of the marudai. Each bundle has been wound onto a weighted bobbin and arranged so that the threads rest over the surface. The braiding is done by repeating the following movements:

The pair of bobbins in the *south* are lifted by resting the threads over the fingers (fig.2).

They are taken across the stool, to the centre of *north* (fig.3).

The outside pair at *north* are lifted (fig.4) and taken to the *south* (fig.5).

The same style of movement is now made in the east-west direction. The pair at *east* are lifted (fig.6) and taken to the centre of *west*.

The outside pair in the *west* are lifted (fig.7) and taken to *east*.

Fig.1

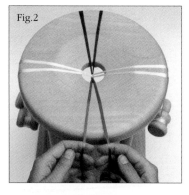

Fig.2

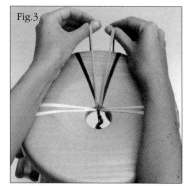

Fig.3

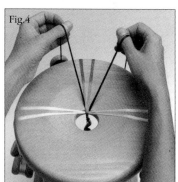

Fig.4

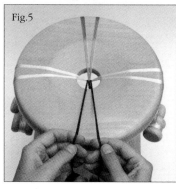

Fig.5

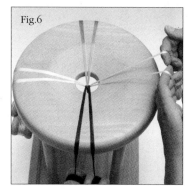

Fig.6

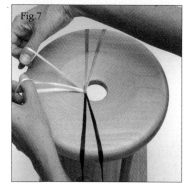

Fig.7

Loop-manipulation

Loop-manipulation is a specific technique where loops of thread are worked together to create a narrow textile. The loops can be held in several ways, over the hands or on individual fingers. The other ends of the loops are secured together at a fixed point. This enables the loops to be pulled away from the fixed point and held under tension. The working process consists of taking one loop either through the inside or around the outside of other loops.

The resulting textile grows away from the fixed point, towards the worker. Short lengths can be tensioned by spreading the arms apart, an action that tightens the *stitches* towards the fixed point. For longer lengths, a beater is required. This can be self-operated equipment, such as the Japanese *ashiuchidai*. Alternatively, an assistant can tighten the stitches as the work progresses. Two or more workers can also co-operate in the loop-manipulating, interchanging the loops between themselves to make larger braids.

Reproductions of 12th and 13th Century braids made using the Japanese technique known as *kute-uchi*.
Courtesy of Masako Kinoshita

A Japanese print inspired by a drawing in a book dating from 1690. It shows a craftsperson working with an *ashiuchidai*, a pivoted wooden beater that is operated by the rope looped around the worker's foot.
Courtesy of Mr Kazuma Mitani.

Many different structures can be created by working with just the loops. Some are made with each side of the loop acting as a separate element. This makes it a fast and efficient method of working because a single action creates the movement of two elements (one for each half of the loop). Others use the whole loop as one element, working them together like free end braiding.

By introducing a weft element, a woven structure (either *plain weave* or *warp-twined*) can be produced. This weft is usually added by a second worker, while the first one manipulates the loops. The weft can also be used to stitch the structure directly onto a garment as work progresses. This method is often used as a decorative hem and can be seen on the Hunza hat from Pakistan.

In Oman, camel reins are traditionally made using a hand-held loop-manipulated braiding technique. Two workers co-operate, one manipulating the loops, whilst the other tensions the stitches.
Courtesy of Gigi Crocker Jones.

A traditional belt from Peru, known as a *chumpi*, is woven using a backstrap. The ends of the warp threads are loop-manipulated to produce several braids that are stitched together to form the end of the belt.
Courtesy of Eiluned Edwards.

Loop-manipulation has undoubtedly been in existence for a long time but evidence is hard to find due to the lack of equipment and the perishable nature of textiles. Although early braids exist that could have been made by loop-manipulation, the first concrete evidence appears to be from a Chinese bronze container, dating from the 1st Century BC. Several figurines on the lid are engaged in textile production and two appear to be loop-manipulating. Later evidence has been discovered in many places throughout the world showing that it was a widespread technique.

Detail of a Chinese bronze cowrie container, dating from the 1st Century BC. The figurines are engaged in textile production and two appear to be loop-manipulating.
Courtesy of Masako Kinoshita.

A Hunza hat with a hem made using loop-manipulation.
Courtesy of Elizabeth Andrews.

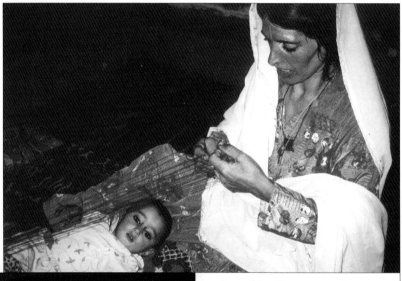

Members of the *Hunza* people from Pakistan. The lady on the right handles the loops whilst the lady on the left introduces a weft and uses this to stitch the resulting band directly onto the rim of a hat.
Courtesy of Ray Napier.

Details from a 17th Century pattern book for loop-manipulated purse strings. This one was hand-written by Lady Bindloss and is illustrated with fine silk samples.
Courtesy of Wigan Archives Service.

How to make a *flat string*.

You will need five loops of thread. The 17th Century *flat string* sample (opposite, bottom left) is made from three loops of red silk and two loops of white silk.

Step 1.

Join the ends of the loops together and attach them to a fixed point so that they can be pulled taut. Arrange the loops on your fingers as shown and note that each loop forms two parts, one *upper shank* and one *lower shank*. For simplicity, each finger will be referred to as letters shown in the photograph.

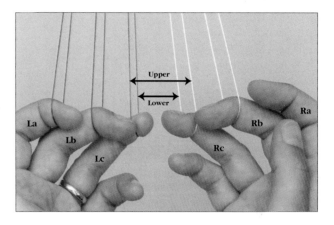

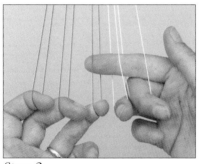

Step 2.
Pass Ra through the loops on Rb and Rc to take hold of the upper shank on Lc.

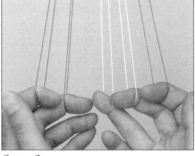

Step 3.
Pull the upper shank of Lc through the loops until it rests on Ra. Spread your arms apart to tension the stitches.

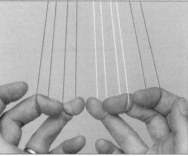

Step 4.
Shift the loop on Lb onto Lc, then shift the loop on La onto Lb.

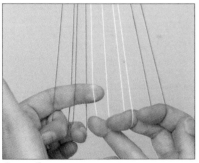

Step 5.
Pass La through the loops on Lb and Lc to take hold of the lower shank on Rc.

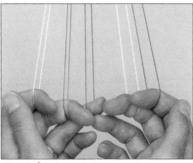

Step 6.
Pull the lower shank of Rc through the loops until it rests on La. This action puts a clockwise twist in the loop. Spread your arms apart to tension the stitches.

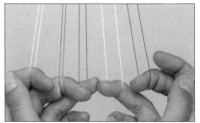

Step 7.
Shift the loop on Rb onto Rc, then the loop on Ra onto Rb. You are now ready to repeat the process from step 2.
Do not worry that the colours are in different positions, they will gradually work back to their original order.

Sprang

Sprang is a term used to describe the process of interworking a set of elements that are secured at both ends. The name derives from the Scandinavian word used to describe their interlinking. The elements can form a flat or circular warp that is usually held taut by a simple frame or between two poles. The elements are taken under or over each other, simultaneously creating two mirror-image structures (one at each end of the work). This is the distinguishing feature of sprang. These two structures will build up until they eventually converge at the mid-point. As they do so, the tension provided by the equipment will need to be eased, to allow for the *take-up* of the elements.

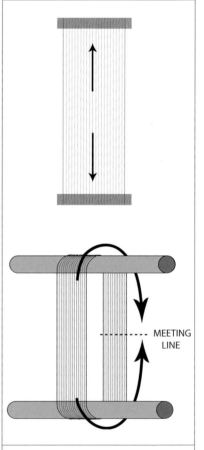

A diagram illustrating the principle of sprang. The elements are held taut at both ends, so that as one element goes over and under the others, two mirror-image structures are simultaneously created.

The work has to be secured at all times so that it cannot unravel. Simply holding the working elements in the hand will do this. Sticks or cords can be temporarily inserted between the elements as work progresses. To finish the work, the elements must be permanently secured. This can be achieved by leaving a final stick or cord in place at the centre of the work. Alternatively, an elastic finish can be created by chaining the elements together and securing with a knot. It is also possible for both pieces of work to be secured separately, and the threads cut across the centre.

A fragment of sprang from Egypt dating to the Coptic period. Most of the elements are interlinking, but others twine round them to form decorative patterns. *Courtesy of Peter Collingwood.*

MEETING LINE

Above: Diagram of a *flat* warp. The elements are manipulated and the results are pushed to the top and bottom of the frame.
Below: Diagram of a *circular* warp. Here, the results are pushed right around the circular warp until they meet, creating a distinctive line.

As with loop-manipulating, sprang is an efficient way of working because a single action accounts for the movement of two parts (the top and bottom half of each element). A direct comparison can be made with a particular form of loop-manipulated braiding where two separate braids are created simultaneously (one behind the other)

One of the earliest surviving examples of sprang is a woman's hair net excavated in Denmark, dating from around 1400 BC. Another early piece dates from 1100 BC and was discovered in Peru. Sprang has been found in many areas and was valued for its ability to make stretchy fabric. Although it is still practised in some areas, its popularity has been superseded by the technique of knitting.

A sprang belt from Pakistan, used as a drawstring for trousers. Most of the belt is plain interlinking but both ends have additional motifs made from carefully sited holes (see detail below left).
It has been made using a circular warp, and the meeting line can be seen at the centre of the belt (see detail above left).
Courtesy of Peter Collingwood.

Dulcelina Suarez, from Santander in
Colombia, making a sprang bag. The warp
is supported on two sticks, one wedged
between the legs of a chair and the other
attached to a belt around her waist.
Other sticks are inserted between the
threads to hold the *stitches* in place.
Courtesy of Linda Mowat.

Sprang bag from Colombia. The bag is *over two, under two*
oblique interlacing (detail below). The handle is made
from a continuous thread that has been worked into three
3-element braids using sprang principles. A weft has been
added at the centre, so that a small section of plain weave
joins the two mirror-image sections together.
Courtesy of Linda Mowat.

An 'in-action' view of sprang.

A warp has been prepared so that an odd number of cotton threads have been secured between two sticks. These will need to be held under tension, as shown on the opposite page. Each row is worked and secured with a temporary stick, which can be removed when several more rows have been completed (fig.1).

The *over two, under two* interlaced structure is worked by starting on the side with the single element. For simplicity, each thread is designated a letter (fig.2).

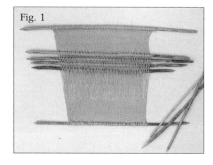

Fig. 1

A goes under **B** and **C** and is lifted with **D** (fig. 3). The left hand holds **AD**, whilst **E** goes under **F** and **G** (fig. 4) and is lifted with **H** (fig. 5).

Work continues in the same manner across to the right, with the left hand holding all of the threads that have been lifted. When a large number of threads have been lifted, a stick can be used to hold open this section whilst work progresses along the row (fig. 6). At the end of the row, the stick is inserted fully so that the hands are free to start working mirror-image movements from right to left.

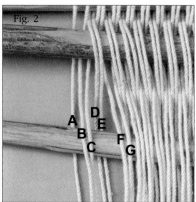

Fig. 2

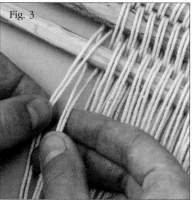

Fig. 3

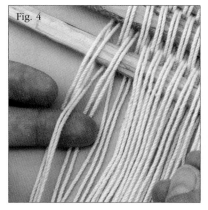

Fig. 4

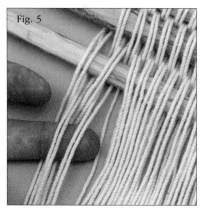

Fig. 5

Fig. 6

Ply-splitting

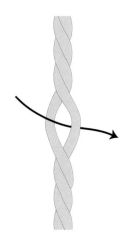

Ply-splitting is the name given to the process by which an element is taken between the plies of another element. Although any plied thread can be used, specially prepared ones produce better results. Cords made from an even number of plies will split equally, giving a balanced result. Also, cords with plenty of twist will firmly hold any elements passing through them. A particular feature of ply-splitting is that it does not require securing whilst work is in progress. Not only does this make it very portable but it also means that it will not unravel in mid-production. Of all the techniques discussed so far, only knotting shares this characteristic.

It is not necessary to have equipment for ply-splitting, though tools are usually used to help draw the working element through the cord being split. Forceps and latchet hooks can be used, as well as tools especially developed for the job, such as the *gripfid*, an adaptation of a splicing tool. A more traditional device is the Indian *gunthani*, a wooden tool with a hole in it, which draws a cord, inserted into the hole, through the cord being split.

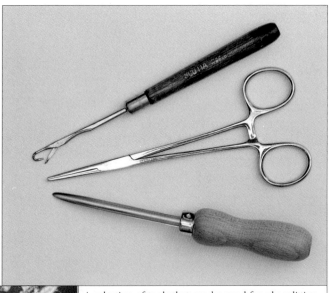

A selection of tools that can be used for ply-splitting: (from top to bottom) a latchet hook, forceps and a Swedish fid.
Courtesy of Edna Gibson.

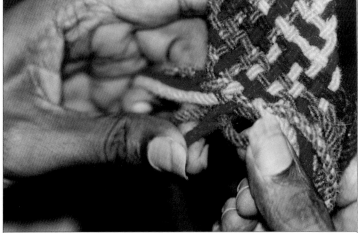

The worker's long fingernails have been used to prise open the ply of the red cord so that the green one can be taken through it.
Courtesy of Errol Pires.

A traditional Indian tool, known as a
gunthani.
Courtesy of Peter Collingwood.

Somabhai Savabhai Rabari, from Gujarat
in India, making a camel girth, known
as a *tang*.
Courtesy of Eiluned Edwards.

Ply-splitting can produce different structures. The most widespread is a warp twined structure which is produced by the process known as *ply-split darning*. Here, one set of elements acts as a warp. These are split by another element that acts as a weft passing through the warp threads at right angles. An example of this can be seen in the *namlo* from Nepal. Alternatively, braid structures can be formed by working a set of elements together, so that all the elements are actively splitting and being split by each other.

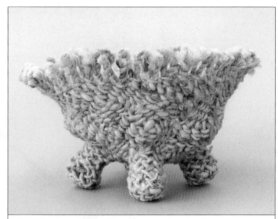

Ply-split vessel made by Peter Collingwood.
Courtesy of Peter Collingwood.

Many variations of ply-split braiding have been developed in north-west India, notably by the Raikas and Rabaris, nomadic camel-breeders by caste occupation. The braids are used as camel trappings and bags, and are traditionally made from goat and camel hair, although cotton is replacing the use of camel hair.

Ply-split braiding is not unique to India but it is not widespread. The Guajiro Indians of Colombia are renowned for their textile work, and they also practise a form of ply-split braiding, using the end products as decorative bridles and cruppers for their donkeys.

Detail of a camel girth. Each element consists of black and white plies. To make the designs, the required colour is bought to the surface, producing a braid structure known as *Two-Layered Oblique Interlacing (TLOI).*
Courtesy of Peter Collingwood.

Above: A Nepalese woman spinning nettle fibre (*allo*) on a drop spindle. This is used for ply-split darning and the making of tumplines (*namlo*) like the one she is wearing on her head, to support her basket.
Courtesy of Veronica Johnston.
Left: Detail of a *namlo.*
Courtesy of Edna Gibson.

Two layered ply-split darning. The black and white layers are interchanged to create the Tibetan motifs.
Courtesy of Gina Corrigan.

Detail of the Tibetan sling on page 31. The band is ply-split darning made from just five cords of undyed yarn.
Courtesy of Gina Corrigan.

How to make a band using ply-split darning.

The band from the end of the Tibetan sling (shown opposite page) is made in undyed yarn but this version uses coloured cotton.

Step 1.

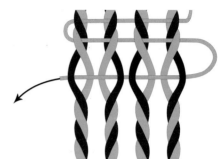

Step 1.
Make two 2-ply, Z-twist cords (as shown on page 11), and two 2-ply, S-twist cords (turn anti-clockwise first, then clockwise). These will be your *warp* cords. Finally make a plain blue 2-ply, Z-twist cord, twice the length of the others. This will be your *weft* cord. Join all five cords together with the longest cord on the left and the other cords alternate 'S' and 'Z'.

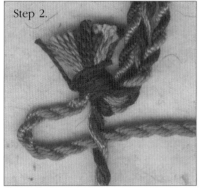

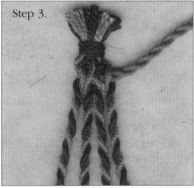

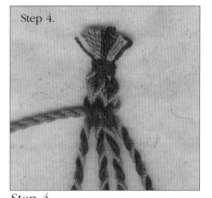

Step 2.
Start close to the join and open the ply of the left-hand warp so that the blue is on top and the navy below. Then thread the weft cord between the two plies, from left to right.

Step 3.
Repeat this until the weft cord has gone from left to right, through all the warp cords.

Step 4.
Now take the weft cord back through the warp cords from right to left. This time open the ply so that the navy is on top and the blue is below. Open the ply close to the previous work so that the plies cross just once between each pass of the weft (see diagram).
Continue working the weft cord back and forth between the plies of the warp cords.

Above: The ply-split darning band.
Below: A ply-split braiding version, made in the same way except instead of always using the *weft*, the left most cord is taken through the other cords, so that each element takes a turn at passing through the others.

Selected Bibliography.

ASHLEY, Clifford W. 1947. *"The Ashley Book of Knots"*. Faber & Faber.

BARBER, Elizabeth JW. 1991. *"Prehistoric Textiles"*. Princeton University Press.

CAHLANDER, Adele. 1980. *"Sling Braids of the Andes"*. Colorado Fibre Centre.

CARDALE-SCHRIMPFF, Marianne. 1972. *"Techniques of Handweaving and allied Arts in Colombia"*, Ph.D(unpubl) Oxford.

CAREY, Jacqui. 1997. *"The Beginner's Guide to Braiding: The craft of Kumihimo"*. Search Press.

COLLINGWOOD, Peter. 1974. *"The Techniques of Sprang"*. Faber & Faber.

COLLINGWOOD, Peter. 1982. *"The Techniques of Tablet Weaving"*. Batsford.

COLLINGWOOD, Peter. 1998. *"The Techniques of Ply-Split Braiding"*. Bellew Publishing.

COLLINGWOOD, Peter. 1998. *"The Maker's Hand"*. Bellew Publishing.

CORRIGAN, Gina. 2001. *"Miao Textiles from China"*. The British Museum Press.

CROCKER JONES, Gigi. 1989. *"Traditional Spinning and Weaving in the Sultanate of Oman"*. Historical Association of Oman.

DIDEROT, Denis. 1751. *"Encyclopedie ou Dictionnaire raisonne des Sciences, des Arts et des Metiers"*. Paris.

DYER, Anne. 1997. *"Purse Strings Unravelled"*. Westhope College.

EMERY, Irene. 1966. *"The Primary Structures of Fabrics"*. The Textile Museum Washington.

GROVES, Sylvia. 1986. *"The History of Needlework Tools"*. Country Life.

HANSON, Egon. 1990. *"Tablet Weaving"*. Hovedland Publishers.

HARRIS, Jennifer. 1993. *"5000 Years of Textiles"*. British Museum Press.

HECHT, Ann. 1989. *"The Art of the Loom"*. British Museum Press.

LEWIS, Paul and Elaine. 1984. *"Peoples of the Golden Triangle"*. Thames and Hudson.

KINOSHITA, Masako. 1994. *"A Study of Archaic Braiding Techniques in Japan"*. Kyoto Shoin.

OWEN, Rodrick. 1995. *"The Big Book of Sling and Rope Braids"*. Cassell.

PARRY, NORMAN & NORMAN, Jennie, Ralph & Ann. 2001. *"Expanding the Girths"*. Sagaman.

ROTH, Walter Edmund. 1970. *"The Arts, Crafts and Customs of the Guiana Indians"*. Johnson Reprint Corporation.

SANCTUARY, Anthony. 1996. *"Rope, Twine and Netmaking"*. Shire Publications Ltd.

SEILER-BALDINGER, Annemarie. 1994. *"Textiles: A Classification of Techniques"*. Crawford House Press.

SPEISER, Noemi. 1983. *"The Manual of Braiding"*. Self published.

SPEISER, Noemi. 2000. *"Old English Pattern Books for Loop Braiding"*. Self published.

VON ELES, Patrizia. 2002. *"Guerriero E Sacerdote. Autorità e comunità nell'età del ferro a Verucchio. La Tomba del Trono."* (Quaderni di Archeologia dell'Emilia Romagna 6). All'Insegna del Giglio

List of participating museums:

The Bowes Museum.
Barnard Castle, County Durham, DL12 8NP. Tel: 01833 690606

Costume and Textile Study Centre, Norfolk Museums and Archaeology Service.
Carrow House, 301 King Street, Norwich, NR1 2TS. Tel: 01603 223870

Newarke Houses Museum.
Leicester, LE2 7BY. Tel: 0116 225 498

Royal Albert Memorial Museum.
Queen Street, Exeter, EX4 3RX. Tel: 01392 265858

Saffron Walden Museum.
Museum Street, Saffron Walden, Essex, CB10 1JL. Tel: 01799 510333

The Wade Costume Collection, Snowshill Manor (the National Trust).
Berrington Hall, Leominister, Herefordshire, HR6 0DW. Tel: 01568 613720

For details about the Braid Society and any further information:

Jacqui Carey: Summercourt, Ridgeway, Ottery St Mary, Devon, EX11 1DT. Tel: 01404 813486